Chanekka Pullens Publishing Presents

DAY ONE

Andre' C. Holder

ISBN: 979-8-218-82558-4

Day One

© 2025 by Andre' C. Holder.

All Rights Reserved.

Published and edited by Chanekka Pullens Publishing

No part of this book may be reproduced or transmitted in any form or by any means, written, electronic, recording, photocopying, or otherwise, without prior written permission of the author, Andre' C. Holder.

For permission requests, solicit the author via the email address below

Andre1104@mademanent007.net

Printed in the United States of America

Table of Contents

1. Anger Issues
2. Insanity
3. Must Been
4. The Growth
5. Opposites
6. What They Don't Know
7. The Mirror Of Me
8. The Star We Are
9. Footnote
10. The Illusion
11. Riddles
12. Prayer
13. Fuel Up
14. Footnote
15. Watch
16. The Mission
17. Reflections (Pointer)
18. Your Own People
19. Spot The Playa Signs
20. Leadership Rules

21. Bout Done
22. Never Limit Your Mind (Outlook)
23. When The Soul Stops Cringing
24. How
25. Joy
26. Never Thought
27. Travels
28. Getting Through It
29. Don't Expect
30. Listen
31. Don't Trip
32. 4 Days 3 Nights
33. Realized
34. Mute
35. To My Son

Anger Issues

Anger issues are very real

People deny their own flaws to cover the disease unknown of

Anger causes death and division

Anger promotes the sickness of the brain which was not diagnosed by professionals

Angry birds (broken women)

- Fatherless
- Hurt
- Confused
- Non-goal-oriented
- Widowed
- Unapologetic

Has a major impact to all Americans worldwide

These worldly taught broken characteristics have shown their faces boldly amongst many communities

Let's fix the uneasy mind of those broken

Let's break the curse to open the door to a more loving culture worldwide

<u>Insanity</u>

Became normal provided by the lack of parenting

Insanity

Made its presence when our ancestors were deprived of the nature of their kingdom

Insanity

Became global from the injustice of a broken system

Insanity

Is hoping the manipulative stops being manipulative

Insanity

Is thinking that someone of a drug using background will change without God

Insanity

Is loving someone who doesn't know how to love

Insanity

Is thinking you are the only one

Insanity

Will eventually show its insanity by not conforming to necessary changes needed to have a healthy oasis.

Insanity

Begins and ends within oneself

Insanity

Is doing the same thing over and over expecting a change; a non-believer

Won't accept to change

Insanity

Is doing everything a person asks of you and not expecting the respect

Of persons needed to be the power necessary in a new becoming

Must Been

Them 5 minutes

Must Been

The way my inner man heals itself daily

Must Been

This few hundred grand I been playing with

Must Been

Surrounding myself with intel that surpassed many comprehended mindsets

Must Been

The way I want to know everything

Must Been

How I'm able to move the way I want to move

Must Been

A vibe not setting right in the universe or individuals' soul

Must Been

How all six senses are all in tune

Must Been

How I asked questions and received meaty answers my whole life

Must Been

The lies told and received within the vessel used to carry to various destination

Must Been

The heart waxing cold towards the overall ending

Must Been

My curiosity which kills access to the cat

Must Been

The lessons taught since 1987

Must Been

In my becoming, in which it's written

Must Been

My loner mannerism vexing greatness

Must Been

Must be

Must Been

The Growth

Came with pain

The Growth

Was dedicating to self

The Growth

Yielded death

The Growth

Made many arguments

The Growth

Departed several relationships

The Growth

Shredded friendships

The Growth

Teaches to manage a harken heart

The Growth

Tested much patience

The Growth

Only smothered the life of happiness

The Growth

Evidently it was too much for them to handle

The Growth

Showed how things can turn for the worse

The Growth

Only grow the seeds planted that desire to grow

The Growth

Opposites

Didn't provide much opposition

Opposites

Led in a way that merged wisdom

Opposites

Taught real men how to be humble

Opposites

Manifested a means of opportunity

Opposites

Brought ops

Opposites

Made a new way of life

Opposites

Attracted the attention away from the union

Opposites

Drove a wedge in between purpose

Opposites

Was the drive that created partial success

Opposites

Let the force decide the fate

Opposites

Developed creativity not made by man

Opposites

Was a working algorithm intended to boycott success

Opposites

Attracted different men and women

Opposites

Road along the side of all negative energy purposed to destroy

Opposites

Are where God receive the most praise

Opposites

Demanded the reason to want clarification

Opposites

Gave the curriculum of global politics

Opposites

Is the exact thing that pulls two people apart from the number one goal of marriage and social bonds

Opposites

One of the main jugular veins of a massive body of people

What They Don't Know

Is it was he that is in me

What They Don't Know

Is what they did not see

What They Don't Know

About Dre' can't hurt him

What They Don't Know

Provided the opportunity to better many that surrounded me

What They Don't Know

Yielded a gap which mastered his ability to foresee the vision

What They Don't Know

Subjected an awe of amazement globally

What They Don't Know

Paved a runway to a development that surpasses supernatural rhythm

What They Don't Know

Pertaining to the skill set acquired, is the gift that comes without repentance

What They Don't Know

War ready adopted the humanity of

What They Don't Know

"You know what you know but seek to know what you don't know."

The Mirror Of Me

Tells the story of me

The Mirror Of Me

Displays the pain inside me

The Mirror Of Me

Hides those imperfections hunting the energy of me

The Mirror Of Me

Hanging on the wall, glaring at many different versions of me

The Mirror Of Me

While gaazing in the eyes of me unlocking neuroplasticity within the spirit of me

The Mirror Of Me

Constantly detouring any forces vexing the darker me

The Mirror Of Me

Which carried me day to day replaying hundreds of thousands of hours of me

The Mirror Of Me

Reflects the complete process in which it takes to be a better me

The Mirror Of Me

The Star We Are

Broken

The Star We Are

Lonely

The Star We Are

Afarid

The Star We Are

Misled

The Star We Are

Confused

The Star We Are

Confined

The Star We Are

Battling addiction

The Star We Are

Defining our definitions of success

The Star We Are

Fearing the unforeseen

The Star We Are

Tempted

The Star We Are

Unfaithful

The Star We Are

Lacking

The Star We Are

Underachieved

The Star We Are

Stagnant

The Star We Are

When prideful

The Star We Are

Fooled

The Star We Are

Misused

The Star We Are

Shines no matter

The Star We Are

Footnote

Having a full spiritual consciousness of manifestation regroups the being that wants righteous formality

"Arise your divine gifts."

- Meditation
- Self-motivation
- Creativity
- Inspiring someone
- Seeking of Wisdom
- Prayer
- Determination

To the reader that's reading this, my intent is as follows:
- Exercise a true sincere blueprint
- Help express growth reform
- Uplift your mind frame in a way that motivates you to pave creativity productivity proactively

The Illusion

Of the way we act

The Illusion

Of which we are paid to act (levels)

The Illusion

Built to distort mass resources

The Illusion

Formatted to wage a war(s)

The Illusion

Severs the supernatural

The Illusion

Take away the zeal of way

The Illusion

Retaining the waters of her (wisdom)

transformation grasped

The Illusion

Shall promote more loving functions

The Illusion

Depicts which chance of ones pathed way

The Illusion

Created is not the one necessarily meant to be

unexampled

The Illusion
Resides rooted within us, the people
The Illusion
Has ultimate ability to fuel change
The Illusion
Is to be sincere amongst all things
The Illusion
Repaired
The Illusion
Fixes
The Illusion
Possess the power of your reform
The Illusion
Has the ability to heal broken homes
The Illusion
Perceived correctly will sponsor unimaginable positivity developing a healthier conscious allowing universe the fair chance of upbringing the whole body of God
The Illusion

Riddles

Full of fiddles

The Riddles

Showing Diddles

Riddles

Fumbling thru the heart

they vibrate effectively

Riddles

Apart of spiritual disguise

Riddles

Systematically advanced with

Riddles

Became trustworthy

Riddles

Determines the aftermath of your survival story

Riddles

Real killers and dealers become businessmen

untraining

Young wig spitters

Riddles

Ion do it for giggles

Riddles

"Please at ease. Isn't no need to tempt me."

Prayer

Cleanse the soul

Prayer

Gives you wisdom

Prayer

Purify the intent of your spiritual purpose

Prayer

Break bondages

Prayer

Promote togetherness

Prayer

Stimulates

Prayer

Determines your future

Prayer

Provides stability

Prayer

Corrects

Prayer

Is effective

Prayer

Created the newness of ministry

Prayer

Saves

Prayer

Will convict

Prayer

Is a meaningful word of righteous faith

Prayer

Has all forms of physical display

Prayer

Can not exist without praise

Prayer

Is key within multiple nationalities

Prayer

Trumps all

"Practice prayer, mean your prayer, learn prayer.

Most of all adopt prayer consistently."

Prayer

Heals hearts

Fuel Up

On your paper routes

Fuel Up

Your mentality

Fuel Up

Desires

Fuel Up

Those vacation spots

Fuel Up

A private jet

Fuel Up

A boss lifestyle

Fuel Up

All relationships

Fuel Up

In action

Fuel Up

On good things

Fuel Up

Your business

Fuel Up

Handling important projects

Fuel Up

In preparation

Fuel Up

With preparation

Fuel Up

Thru the energy of adoration

Fuel Up

On zeal

Fuel Up

Your tenacity

Fuel Up

Undeniable faith

Fuel Up

Life

Fuel Up

Giving

Fuel Up

Being kind

Fuel Up

At helping those in need

Fuel Up

With love

Fuel Up

<u>Footnote</u>

Everyday has been a constant battle in my becoming
I know sometimes all things seem as if I completely got it together
However, that is not the case at all
Bestowing a mass wealth of knowledge, with the intent to distribute
Life is very essential
I've been through hell (traumas) my human instinct is self-protection
Which causes me to shut out those hurts
Either I'm going to totally not care (mentally block out)
Or become silent and reach out to pull up a new nation of people who want the information of this memorable history

Watch

Patterns

Watch

Facials

Watch

Emotions

Watch

Tears

Watch

Pain

Watch

Your woman

Watch

Your man

Watch

How the energy be

Watch

The opportunities you allow others to do

Watch

Your money

Watch

Enemies

Watch

Fake people

Watch

How you give access to yourself

Watch

Time

Watch

Because you know to watch

Watch

The phony

Watch

The addiction of adrenaline

Watch

A hater

Watch

People

Watch

Body language

Watch

How things play out

Watch

Listen. Look. Learn

Watch

How God solves any problem you may have

Watch

And knowing what isn't seen does not

mean they are not watching

Watch

Fake love

Watch

Sneaky individuals

Watch

Those that never do wrong

Watch

Karma

Watch

A gambler

Watch

An observer

Watch

Your children

Watch

The inconsistency of others

Watch

Idle time havers

Watch

Me

Watch

Just

Watch

The Mission

Is to love one another

The Mission

Was laid out on the platform to enhance our humanity

The Mission

Reflects

The Mission

Can be delayed

The Mission

Will drive you

The Mission

Sometimes overwhelms many

The Mission

When adopted becomes a divine fight

The Mission

Belittle the weak

The Mission

Formulate

The Mission

Shows self-awareness

The Mission

Not impossible

The Mission

Balances

The Mission

Holds the power to expose people's intent

The Mission

Restores confidence

The Mission

Is the reason the addict recovered

The Mission

Can be aborted

The Mission

Gathers intel

The Mission

Uplifts greatness

The Mission

Performs rare morals

The Mission

Is set to examine the unknown self

The Mission

Will reunite family

The Mission

Helped those get through prison time

The Mission

Caused that wanted weight loss

The Mission

Caused someone insanity

The Mission

Help master abilities to focus

The Mission

Connected all members of the body to produce the better you by being on a mission reading this book

The Mission

Supplements

The Mission

Is Royal

The Mission

Subjects to missions

The Mission

Is indeed to express operations

The Mission

Been the mission

"I speak success over your mission no matter what that is."

Reflection (Pointer)

Knowing within that I'm not perfect in a world of
believers that diagnoses themselves as perfect.
It is our duty to become
real with ourselves within your personal life
situations
It's imperative that we as a body of upcoming
pillars in society take the
moment to promote the simple creativity and
display regulations out in
the universe by artistic abilities given by God
This Project was and is the product of time
management, determination, an idea, motivation,
vision, dedication, commitment
Outreach ministry
Most importantly, I thank God for the willingness
spirit, the spirit of
obedience and the tenacity to give His people a
word

Your Own People

Will snake you

Your Own People

Will make you feel less than

Your Own People

Jealous of you

Your Own People

Will steal from you

Your Own People

Have double standards on how they treat you

Your Own People

Hate you

Your Own People

Play both sides

Your Own People

Won't give you props they know you deserve

Your Own People

Gone fade your ole lady

Your Own People

Not going to understand your light

Your Own People

Wanna see you lose
Your Own People
Envy your accomplishments
Your Own People
Will set you up
Your Own People
Acting
Your Own People
Can never take accountability
Your Own People
Can't tell you they're sorry
Your Own People
Not resourceful
Your Own People
Gone drain your energy
Your Own People
Can't take good advice
Your Own People
Slander your name
Your Own People
Procrastinate
Your Own People

Never tell the 100 percent truth

Your Own People

Use you

Your Own People

Lack communication

Your Own People

Playa Signs

I. The brush off
II. The silent phone
III. The not wanting to be touched
IV. The turned over phone
V. The get home and go sit on the toilet
VI. The extra set of clothes in the car
VII. The changing of appearance suddenly
VIII. The always angry character
IX. The asking why you rush home
X. The quick to leave (abandoning problems)
XI. The omittance (not telling the whole truth)
XII. The disconnection of spirituality
XIII. The I don't want to be bothered
XIV. The grudge holder
XV. The manipulator
XVI. The quite innocence (freak)

XVII.	The smooth talker
XVIII.	The Iphone user
XIX.	The Snapchat user
XX.	The liar
XXI.	The never do nothing wrong
XXII.	The mind game player
XXIII.	The Black broken (man/woman)

Leader Rules

I. Love thyself
II. Stay away from low vibrational people
III. Time management with excellent choice making skills
IV. Never lose sight of the goals
V. Choose your team wisely
VI. Grind hard
VII. Adapt to whatever an individual proclaims you to be
VIII. Dislike a draining, easily swayed, and undecided woman
IX. Hang with all levels of all types of people (33% of time w/poor people, 33% of time w/middle class people, 33% of time w/rich people)
X. Never chase woman/man (major flaw of mine)

XI. Manage how you let people use you
XII. Always invest
XIII. Understand it's more hurtful days caused by others under your leadership
XIV. Study about how to "read people"
XV. Always solve problems for long days

Bout Done

She is

Bout Done

It is

Bout Done

We is

Bout Done

The way we is

Bout Done

With a lot of things

Bout Done

Going through mental shit

Bout Done

With pleasing and not being acknowledged

Bout Done

Living for other people

Bout Done

Hoping in perfect love

Bout Done

Many say "told"

Bout Done

Ran her course

Bout Done

Of being in a committed relationship

Bout Done

With me

Bout Done

Why you still with me

Bout Done

Scripting my role

Bout Done

Pouring

Bout Done

Motivating

Bout Done

Sharing

Bout Done

Being a dummy

Bout Done

Roaring

Bout Done

Being loved

Bout Done

Broken

Bout Done

Explaining

Bout Done

Of unwanted headaches

Bout Done

Being victimized still after God saved me

Bout Done

With entitlement(s)

Bout Done

Giving all of me

Bout Done

Letting my peers lower my vibrations

Bout Done

Taking lack of respect

Bout Done

Fought a fight

Bout Done

Never Limit Your Mind (Outlook)

It's a terrible thing to waste what's bringing it to life by expressing my bigger hurdles on paper so that those would know how I

strive daily to stay grounded

My life has been a testimonial and still I battle with fear, depression, sex addiction, and many other things that may not be displayed on my social media

Accepting my savior catapulted me into a new way of moving

I changed up on many people and I know it was unfair or hurtful; I apologize

to all those I couldn't reach, teach, or keep my promises to.

The purpose leads as the leading algorithm which inspired this project

I desire to reach as many as I can. I hope whoever reads this book gets something out of it.

Life lessons, experience, and good parents crafted me to my becoming.

Never limit yourself to things not righteous.

It took me a long time and many mistakes to develop and have contentment for the people

Never look backward at the past but learn to forgive your spouse, baby mother, baby daddy, girlfriend, boyfriend, mother, father, granny, aunt, pastor, doctor, uncle, Mother Mary Ann, Joe, and anyone who wronged you.

Hate is a cancer. You will find yourself destroying all the things worth having because the cancer is eating your soul away.

With God and an ear that waits on the lord, you will be carried through your life burdens and hurdles

When The Soul Stops Cringing

It's done

When The Soul Stops Cringing

Execute the ending

When The Soul Stops Cringing

Create a new beginning

When The Soul Stops Cringing

Be steadfast

When The Soul Stops Cringing

Watch; I repeat watch

When The Soul Stops Cringing

Seek the guidance needed

When The Soul Stops Cringing

Read

When The Soul Stops Cringing

Refill your temple of life

When The Soul Stops Cringing

In some cases, some reached their ending

Has your soul stopped cringing

How

A person says they love you but can't show it

How

We epically sexing everyday then arguing the same day

How

I made it; I personally couldn't say it was me alone

How

When love dies, we turn to a blind eye

How

The hell is trusting a deal breaker, and your partner can't be trusted

How

Do we expect change but will not accept our flaws

How

Do we judge the next person and not completely secure in ourselves

How

Do people down the same person they secretly mimicking

How

Does one part their lips, mind, or etc… to belittle anyone that is operating for you

How

Does the past continue to be present in your future we claim to be moving forward from

How

Do we expect God to restore our being and not allow Him to use His angels in place to show you the flaws

How

Can we benefit from every resource then still have a broken spirit

How

Do humans complain about the future comings and always mad at their spouse, partner, or mentor because they must change

How

Have we been allowed to play both sides throughout the centuries

How

Can God work in situations where the parties involved are pulling in separate directions

How

Just tell me

How

Can a king lead the kingdom without love from its queen of that kingdom

How

Has brokenness taken over our minds when we have been taught a made-up version of our existing being

How

Do we know love and its entirety that's barely truly received within our culture

How

Does the healing supposed to come about

How

Much time do we have

How

Before the earth herself gives up

How

Is lack of communication the leading issue in our community

How

Is life being given when negativity is the only characteristic chosen to live by

How

Did we become an addict to one another only to grow to hate one another

How

Do we look anybody in the eye and lie straight faced

How

Oh

How

Must I teach so that I can reach the soul's heavenly father

How

Do I explain

How

Shall I even complain

How

When they love you correctly

How

Tell me

How

And I stood on ten toes

How

Did lack of trust continue to plague our very union

How

Must I achieve

How

Must we rectify the independence formulated

among our peers

How

Easy was it to cast all your burdens on God and allow Him to work it out

How

Did it make you feel

How

Damaged do you think the others are

How

Can't you see the loving soul that speaks to you in the calm still voice saying relax

How

How is an adverb which could go on and on throughout the brain or anything else it may consume

"The sum of my How's"

Joy

Came this morning

Joy fulfilled our purpose

Joy

Oh, my soul

Joy

Amongst my frenemies

Joy

Walking into the new

Joy

Learn

Joy

Welcomed

Joy

Oh, joy

Joy

In the living room as I create this healing

Joy

When the universe seems not to promote your hopes

Joy

Record less

Joy

Sat aside

Joy

Flowing in the soul

Joy

To your accomplishments

Joy

Through your trails

Joy

Until the coming of God

Joy

When we walk

Joy

When we talk

Joy

Undefeated

Joy

With unbreakable mercy

Joy

Mastering mental health

Joy

In marriages

Joy

Overrunning

Joy

Led into the next generations to come

Joy

Molding healthier relationships

Joy

Over your life

Joy

Shut in your bones

Joy

Visualizing heaven

Joy

Subsiding police brutality

Joy

Our ancestors had to enforce that change

Joy

Not taken for granted

Joy

Should trump all emotions

Joy

Within

Joy

Tells the pure unadulterated truth

Joy

Explains

Joy

Create understanding

Joy

Comes in a bundle

Joy

Joyfully

Joy

In every season

Joy

When you inhale

Joy

When you exhale

Joy

Was

Joy

Is

Joy

Will come

Joy

Hopefully, one day joy will overtake the suppressed anger hidden out of souls

Never Thought

I would be happy

Never Thought

My time would come

Never Thought

I would be a single father

Never Thought

Bout how influential I am

Never Thought

Success covered me

Never Thought

I was this wealthy

Never Thought

We would master certain areas of this life

Never Thought

My same day ones would still be here

Never Thought

Love would love me despite of

Never Thought

My upbringing would carry me

Never Thought

One day I would be without my father and mentor

Never Thought

I would be one of the most valuable people in America

Never Thought

About being a full-time drug dealer (nope)

Never Thought

Kia wouldn't be here after 2018

Never Thought

I deserved to be different in my own way

Never Thought

My mentality would have swayed (slightly)

Never Thought

It would be my reasonable duty managing a new generation

Never Thought

That relationships had a limit to seduction

Never Thought

Mixed emotions would come from the ones I loved most

Never Thought

People gone be people

Never Thought

About the flip side of others' minds which could have two sides

Never Thought

My people would be the laziest nation(s)

Never Thought

Sex could become the issue of any union

Never Thought

Boredom fuels sinful acts

Never Thought

Why

Never Thought

God would come to me personally

Never Thought

I would live in the matrix

Never Thought

I would be filled with the holy ghost and fire

Never Thought

Travels

Across the nation

Travels

Amongst the creativity in your mind

Travels

Before the beginning of time

Travels

Abroad

Travels

Networking at your fingertips

Travels

Of the past

Travels

Soothing the present moment

Travels

Collecting culture every place visited

Travels

Developed commonwealth

Travels

Were the recipes which we are

Travels

Complimented history

Travels

Thru time

Travels

In planning

Travels

Already conquered

Travels

Not yet explored

Travels

In the eyes of the soul

Travels

On the C17

Travels

Of laughter

We all travel daily; seize the moments of

Travel

Getting Through It

Gone be a mental challenge

Getting Through It

Battling thru a slew of emotions

Getting Through It

Been a fight that shows the cougar

Getting Through It

Many nights alone crippled zeal

Getting Through It

Made me cry, hurt, and question everybody

Getting Through It

When not trusting anybody tears a hole in our soul

Getting Through It

Only proves that change can be mastered provided sacrifice burdens you for the journey

Getting Through It

Stimulates peace

Getting Through It

Manipulates the essence in which time travels freely

Getting Through It

Causes individuals to become great pioneers

Getting Through It

May trick the minds patterns of development

Getting Through It

Changed, change, or changes the scenario in which a person view, views, and or handle

freedom

Getting Through It

Suppose to reflect strength

Getting Through It

Evidently triggers pain

Getting Through It

Possibly wages war between good and evil thoughts

Getting Through It

Helps certain aspects in spirituals walks to either crash or prosper

Getting Through It

Lord knows for 30 plus years, I've been going through it

Getting Through It

Right now, with tears streaming at this very moment, allows the pressure to release chemicals that curve toxicity within our trillions of cells infrastructure

Don't Expect

To make everyone happy

Don't Expect

For everyone to praise your move

Don't Expect

That which your mind expects

Don't Expect

Anyone to see things the way you do

Don't Expect

Great days everyday

Don't Expect

Love the way you give it

Don't Expect

The world to embrace your flaws

Don't Expect

Nothing that compliments your position more than some else's

Don't Expect

Life to be easy

Don't Expect

Riches without pain close

Don't Expect

Something out of nothing 99% of your time

Don't Expect

Anything someone doesn't have, known, or seen

Don't Expect

Loved ones to understand the suffering you suffer

Don't Expect

100% so that let downs will not be a hard attack on your body

Don't Expect

Your spouse or partner to be the one that knows you the most

Don't Expect

Happiness when many are surviving off hurt

Don't Expect

Everything to go according to plan

Don't Expect

Investments to thrive fast pace

Don't Expect

A calm soul while nesting an uneasy soul

Don't Expect

Being giving anything without great responsibility

Don't Expect

Partnership with an independent that succeeded off pure survival

Don't Expect

Life without life lifing

Don't Expect

Loyalty from people or persons who do not know your definition of circumstances that defined a persons loyalty

Don't Expect

Peace

Don't Expect

Life forever

Don't Expect

Certain relationships to last forever

Don't Expect

A perfect person, place, or thing

Don't Expect

Wisdom from a light reader

Don't Expect

It

Don't Expect

No one to build on to a solid foundation when they're trying to establish one of their own

Don't Expect

Success without a series of tests

Don't Expect

Time to be a main factor of any relationship

Don't Expect

A settling for less type of person

Don't Expect

If you won't look for it

Don't Expect

Saints to be Saints

Don't Expect

Heaven vibrating at a hellish mind state

Don't Expect

Forever

Don't Expect

For others to understand the joy within themselves

Don't Expect

Humans plus unlimited time the praise to equal total happiness of unity

Don't Expect

Sanity in majority of humanity

Don't Expect

Gifts

Don't Expect

Acceptance

Don't Expect

Help

Don't Expect

Them to realize the boundaries in the respect of in someone who doesn't have respect

Don't Expect

"Life has a way of conning you, distracting you, and most of all, sneaking up on you. Read more, meditate frequently, and possess the power that has the ability of renewing the acceptance."

Listen

To what people say

Listen

To the heart

Listen

Life will expose the true way

Listen

To understand meaning

Listen

And be slow to speak

Listen

So the soul will grow

Listen

To your parents

Listen

To listen

Listen

To hear

Listen

To understand

Listen

For the mind's sake

Listen

Because words have a way of expressing themselves

Listen

To receive harmony

Listen

In the morning

Listen

In the noon day

Listen

At dawn

Listen

Before bed

Listen

So that the 3rd eye will activate consciousness while sleep

Listen

To the children

Listen

To the still voice of the lord

Listen

And relax

Listen

For the restoration of the soul

Listen

When don't want to be bothered

Listen

Through interpreting dreams

Listen

To individuals when speaking out of anger

Listen

With an open heart

Listen

With restriction knowing your intent

Listen

Oh, people listen

Don't Trip

When they don't talk

Don't Trip

In their absence

Don't Trip

Over spoiled milk

Don't Trip

Over untied shoes

Don't Trip

Just flip

Don't Trip

God repairs

Don't Trip

Attract

Don't Trip

Manifest

Don't Trip

Universe provides

Don't Trip

They will follow the path necessary

Don't Trip

Time fixes all

Don't Trip

Too deep

Don't Trip

Over ending situations

Don't Trip

Cause individuals lack

Don't Trip

When structure is not accepted

Don't Trip

It's all good

Don't Trip

Your time coming

Don't Trip

Opinions are like assholes

Don't Trip

Replace

Don't Trip

Pray

Don't Trip

Allocate revenue

Don't Trip

Over woman

Don't Trip

Over men

Don't Trip

Over failure

Don't Trip

When your car breaks down

Don't Trip

When life sale you frown

Don't Trip

Be you

Don't Trip

Live for you

Don't Trip

How they feel about cha

Don't Trip

People lost

Don't Trip

Excuses only cause procrastination

Don't Trip

Gotta be a better situation

Don't Trip

You are stronger than most

Don't Trip

Pick up your lips

Don't Trip

Care less about that BS

Don't Trip

The children counting on you

Don't Trip

Most of the love given not real

Don't Trip

I'm telling you firsthand DON'T TRIP

4 Days 3 Nights

Of fun

4 Days 3 Nights

Going through several emotions

4 Days 3 Nights

In which I predicted

4 Days 3 Nights

God kept me

4 Days 3 Nights

Made history

4 Days 3 Nights

With ill will

4 Days 3 Nights

Alone

4 Days 3 Nights

Plenty of time to think

4 Days 3 Nights

Ain't no telling

4 Days 3 Nights

Realized

What I meant

Realized

How to move after that event

Realized

That it's not worth the trouble

Realized

Real eyes recognize real lies

Realized

How strong a man, the man can be

Realized

Motive

Realized

What is not

Realized

God is really moving

Realized

Weakness

Realized

The power

Realized

That people gone move how they want

Realized

Who not real

Realized

Can not put anything past people

Realized

The full realm of hatred

Realized

Where trauma will end

Realized

Setbacks came from overly caring

Realized

Definition of stressful

Realized

This part of my life is by far the roughest patch

Realized

Level of toleration

Realized

What was done is done

Realized

I can survive

Realized

Death eats at the living daily by situations

Realized

Lesson learned

Realized

Position

Realized

Worth

Realized

What

Realized

A strong hold

Realized

My personal addiction

Realized

I don't need to manage

Realized

The word with the worldly experience

Realized

Why I cry

Realized

The root of the demise

Realized

Family is the purest form of sanity

Realized

No matter the lesson, it's always a blessing

Realized

Aye, Dre', keep your eyes on the prize

Realized

No matter how rough life gets, it's joy in the morning

Realized

The plot was blaming the situation to accomplish desired objectives

Realization

It's near the ending

Mute

Your mind

Mute

Speech

Mute

To listen

Mute

Organizes confusion

Mute

Create understanding

Mute

Shows elevation

Mute

The chaos

Mute

Your TV for awhile

Mute

The hearts longing

Mute

Be All You Can Be

Be All You Can Be

Pastors

Be All You Can Be

Leaders

Be All You Can Be

My sons

Be All You Can Be

Preachers

Be All You Can Be

Ladies

Be All You Can Be

Gentlemen

Be All You Can Be

Doctors

Be All You Can Be

Readers

Be All You Can Be

Deacons

Be All You Can Be

Soldiers

Be All You Can Be

Biden

Be All You Can Be

Citizens

Be All You Can Be

Family

Be All You Can Be

Hurting

Be All You Can Be

Sick

Be All You Can Be

Married folk

Be All You Can Be

Through all

Be All You Can Be

Fed up

Be All You Can Be

Battling addiction

Be All You Can Be

Because it's possible

Be All You Can Be

Life's short

Be All You Can Be

In hope

Be All You Can Be

Struggling

Be All You Can Be

Ye that's depressed

Be All You Can Be

State leaders

Be All You Can Be

Railway workers

Be All You Can Be

Transit workers

Be All You Can Be

Judges

Be All You Can Be

District Attorneys

Be All You Can Be

Policemen

Be All You Can Be

Waitresses

Be All You Can Be

Governors

Be All You Can Be

Vice Presidents

Be All You Can Be

CEOs

Be All You Can Be

Janitors

Be All You Can Be

Senior Citizens

Be All You Can Be

Fishermen

Be All You Can Be

Owner operators

Be All You Can Be

You college students

Be All You Can Be

Pilots

Be All You Can Be

Air traffic controllers

Be All You Can Be

Firemen

Be All You Can Be

NASCAR drivers

Be All You Can Be

Mothers

Be All You Can Be

Cousins

Be All You Can Bes

Unks

Be All You Can Be

Auntie

Be All You Can Be

Mentors

Be All You Can Be

Botanists

Be All You Can Be

Scientists

Be All You Can Be

Poor

Be All You Can Be

Rich

Be All You Can Be

Determining your move in life

Be All You Can Be

Even as you seem to lose

Be All You Can Be

In the hustle

Be All You Can Be

Artists

Be All You Can Be

Ghost writers

Be All You Can Be

Even if your partner cheating

Be All You Can Be

Learning new intelligence

Be All You Can Be

When you travel

Be All You Can Be

Consistently

Be All You Can Be

Chefs

Be All You Can Be

Seek to achieve

Be All You Can Be

Let nothing but God bring you to your knees

Be All You Can Be

Shoot for the stars

Be All You Can Be

No road traveled is too far

To My Sons

Grind until you're successful

To My Sons

I love y'all

To My Sons

I done my best

To My Sons

Never let anybody set you back

To My Sons

A man that doesn't work doesn't eat

To My Sons

I apologize for being in the streets too much

To My Sons

I'm proud of the guys you are

To My Sons

If I ever parish, make me proud

To My Sons

Respect the women that respect you

To My Sons

Save your revenue

To My Sons

Invest your capital

To My Sons

Buy stocks

To My Sons

Listen to your mothers

To My Sons

Forgive those that misuse you

To My Sons

Never be a fool to anyone

To My Sons

Be anything you're determined to be

To My Sons

Don't have more than two children

To My Sons

Train your children in the way they should go

To My Sons

Be creative in order to make a living

To My Sons

Love your grandmothers

To My Sons

Have a 1 on 1 relationship with God

To My Sons

Be better than me

To My Sons

Live life don't let life stress you

To My Sons

Hold on to all antiques acquired

To My Sons

Buy gold

To My Sons

Buy silver

To My Sons

Master English

To My Sons

Know you were created out of love

To My Sons

Never be in unhappy relationships

To My Sons

Don't gamble

To My Sons

A wise man leaves an inheritance to his children children's children

To My Sons

Have your own everything in your name

To My Sons

Do not live life in debt to no bank, man, or program

To My Sons

Read more

To My Sons

Want to know your family tree history

To My Sons

Obey the laws of the land to your best ability

To My Sons

Research all things before indulging into

To My Sons

Sex is not everything

To My Sons

Be with a woman that wants the same things you want out of life

To My Sons

Marry only one time

To My Sons

If ever get put on child support, pay now not later

To My Sons

Be men of your word

To My Sons

Attend church at least one or two times a month

To My Sons

Never "Keep up with the Jones's," as the elderly would say

To My Sons

"Never take any wooden nickels," as stated by Great grandfather Samuel Holder Jr.

To My Sons

I won't be here forever but know that I'm with you in spirit and in a righteous lifestyle

To My Sons

Take heed to corrective criticism

To My Sons

It's okay to cry when life gets hard

To My Sons

Everything I tried to do was to make sure you were set up for success

To My Sons

Good social relationships with people like minded people are better than money

To My Sons

Always have a stash of money set aside for lawyers

To My Sons

Always pray at least five times a day

To My Sons

The right way is the hardest way to live but the most rewarding

To My Sons

Trust your conscious (still voice of right doings)

To My Sons

Follow God

To My Sons

Read all religious bibles for infrastructure of how to live

To My Sons

Do not be attached to ungrateful women

To My Sons

Be able to take care of yourself without anybody's help before deciding to marry

To My Sons

Before you marry, get to know your spouse's family to see if that's what you want to be a part of the rest of your lives

To My Sons

Be around the people you attract not the ones you want to be around

To My Sons

If a woman cheat, never allow her more than two times to betray you

To My Sons

Learn to cook

To My Sons

Be clean

To My Sons

Take care of your hygiene

To My Sons

Try not to argue with women

To My Sons

Only have one credit card

To My Sons

If you can't buy something three times you can't afford it

To My Sons

If you fail pick yourself up and try again

To My Sons

Never be a quitter at things you want that will better your circumstances

To My Sons

You guys are the best assets I have ever acquired in this lifetime

To My Sons

I'm proud of the men you are now (6/26/2024)

To My Sons

Take good care of the things you purchase

To My Sons

Mingle with different cultures

To My Sons

If you're capable, learn different languages

To My Sons

Work for someone else for a little while but become your own boss

To My Sons

The streets don't love you

To My Sons

Never let anybody trick you out your spot (any situation applied to)

To My Sons

Be meek

To My Sons

Humble yourselves

To My Sons

Be a collector of antiques (20 plus year old collectables)

To My Sons

Master time management

To My Sons

Keep the legacy alive

Dedication

I want to thank everyone who supported this book.

My mission is to reach as many as I can, showing righteous and real-life words that keep me going. I want to thank my parents Wilhelmina Brenda Holder and Andre' Carteous Vaughn for not aborting me - giving me a chance at being the individual God designed me to be. I also want to thank my sister Shekia Monique Jiles for being there for me when I needed her most.

"I MISS YOU!" To all my family that loved me unconditionally as a Jit (young fella), I love you all dearly.

A special shout out to heaven to my grandparents Brenda Holder, Samuel Holder Jr., Bobby Jean Doston, and Robert Hatchet for creating my parents so that I may be in the land of the living.

I want to thank all of my friends for holding me down through the gaps when I was out in the streets as a young man. Slim, CJ Hustlers, Ray Ray, Slickshit, Dee, Shafique Islam, Turd "Shon Gotti", "Shafali" Aziza Islam, Shawn Islam, Fazia Islam, Dr. Martha J. Thomas, "Doc" John R. Thomas, Fran Sweatt, Denise Holder (auntie), Marcus J. Thomas, "Bipu" Rezual Karim, (UK) Dr. Alice Baily and a slew of others that played a major role in my becoming.

    I want to give a personal warming to Canisha Denise Alred for sticking around for nine years. She stayed around and was a rock in my becoming. She put up with a lot dealing with a (Hood Star) like me. I put that woman through the test of time.

    To everyone else that I may have missed or didn't call out, I personally want to say, "I appreciate you more than you know." To DeMarcus Amos, Treaunus Alred, and Treaston Alred continue to strive toward greatness and take care of your mom as time moves forward. "Jenny Black" Hull you know we locked in for life, OG. Love! "Lucy" Jalisa Alred, fam, you know you locked in on gang and nem. Keep growing and holding down them kids like you do so well.

To my inspiration Ayanna Holder and Keyanna Holder, I adore you guys more than you will ever know. I am proud to have you ladies as my sisters. God himself sent you two to slow me down and that you beautiful ladies done flawlessly. I owe you young ladies my life.

This quick read is for all walks of life, races, and genders. My hope is that the readers take something out of these real-life experiences and apply them to their daily life as building blocks and moral support. Everything outlined, titled, created has been pillars and strategies used to carry me three decades.

Most, if not all of these manuscripts within this project are based on real life events and stories. I dedicated myself to the commitment of creating something to give back to the community. Every word was given to me as I wrote this on a daily. Meaning meditation and thought was the leader of this project.

None of these poems, footnotes, and motivational quotes were pre thought out. I wanted to give from the heart, mind, and soul. I wanted this first project to be authentic and the truth. All this material was and is my own creation. This amazing creation was not discussed with anyone before its beginning.

The Holy Spirit assisted me along the way. A lot of prayer, growth, and discipline complimented the process. Andre' Holder never thought that one day I would create the time to complete this. I was always on the go, in the streets, or giving time to others trying to solve world problems. What makes me qualified to reach out to Gods own people is my journey to whom I've become over the course of 37 years. You are not alone when it comes to the dynamic of things I have accomplished internationally, locally, and domestically. A lot of the time I cannot believe the things I have done.

However, I want to give all the credit to God because without Him I am nothing. It was Him that carried me out of wickedness into a well-preserved light of change. Not me! I was willing and He did the rest.

The title of this is "Day One" because no matter my hardship, anger, loneliness, ups, downs, setbacks, losses, short-comings, sins, and/or anything that was designed to make me a failure, I have overcome it. For me, my "DAY ONE" was September 17th, 2005, the day I accepted The Holy Ghost as the ruler and master of my life.

When Is your Day One?

Do you remember your Day One?

And if so, please remember that you too are a part of Gods Day One.

Written by: Andre' C. Holder

Published by: Chanekka Pullens Publishing

Contact: 615-579-0774

Email: Andre1104@mademanent007.net

6339 charlotte Pike

Suite 827

Nashville, TN 37209

www.ingramcontent.com/pod-product-compliance
Lightning Source LLC
Chambersburg PA
CBHW071216160426
43196CB00012B/2328